FROM IDEA TO DIGITAL PRODUCT

HOW TO SUSTAIN GREAT INSPIRATIONS
TO AVOID HIDDEN AND INEVITABLE RISKS
OF FAILURE

Ivan Trajkovic

First edition. June 26, 2019.
Written by Ivan Trajkovic.
Cover Design: Ivan Agency.
https://ivan.agency

CONTENTS

In gratitude   *viii*
Introduction   *1*

Life experiences influence our work creations   *5*
Diverse value of digital transformation   *13*

12-milestone methodology for digital product concepting   *16*
Milestone 1   *21*
Milestone 2   *24*
Milestone 3   *32*
Milestone 4   *38*
Milestone 5   *42*
Milestone 6   *45*
Milestone 7   *47*
Milestone 8   *52*
Milestone 9   *56*
Milestone 10   *59*
Milestone 11   *63*
Milestone 12   *68*

The execution   *70*
From idea to digital product: final note   *72*

For Petra and Klara

"A digital product is born from a spark of geniosity, better known as an idea. The transformation of this idea into a digital product is the process that can destine it to success or failure."

Ivan Trajkovic

IN GRATITUDE

This book is a culmination of a series of events that took place in the past ten years. Upon returning to Serbia in 2008 after having graduated from NSU in Fort Lauderdale with a degree in CIS and having worked as a software engineer for Monster.com and BWIN.com, I don't have a better explanation of the situation than a common scenario back home – I was overqualified for the then domestic IT sector. There were a handful of software development companies working internationally, and I could not even get a job interview. By the way, prior to that, I had just delivered an API for the new live betting system for EuroCup 2008 for BWIN.com as a tech lead. The new version performed perfectly and the betting tickets closure rate, along with the company profits, increased dramatically.

I was annoyed by the political situation and empty words, and, being bold by nature, I responded to a news article by the Ministry of Telecommunications and IT about the return of youth that gained education around the world to their home country. It was very shocking to get a response; a few days later, I was an advisor to the minister, and as the position was quite intriguing, I declined an offer that I got in the meantime that was four times the average software engineer salary in Belgrade at the time. I wanted to change things, I wanted to make a mark, and I took it upon myself to lead a child safety on the Internet campaign which was very well-received across the country. I wanted to take things to the next level as I was also involved in one of the first eGovernment projects in the country, and therefore prepared an Open Source Government strategy for Serbia based on the UK Open Source Government strategy. Young and inexperienced, I was stupid to believe it was in the government's interest to save the taxpayers' money, and while my strategy ended up in the trash, I also had the chance to realize how millions of euros of the taxpayers' money go to waste just for the sake of spending the entire budget. During the time I spent working for the ministry, I founded the first Serbian finTech startup Ustedi.rs (eng. Save.rs) which was a comparison engine for banks' loan offers for personal banking. Unfortunately, it was also ahead of its time and I shut it down.

With my first daughter born and the second one on the way, I decided to quit my job in the ministry, having witnessed the aforementioned. I guess luck follows the fools and the brave, and just days after I quit, I got a project from London that I could deliver myself alone in only three months, but it would earn me a yearly ministry-range salary. One thing lead to another and, three years later, I exceeded sole agency trading limits by 700% while averaging sixteen hours of work per day in three years straight. Engineers Ltd were born. That was all made possible due to my loving wife and my dear parents-in-law who took on themselves the burden of raising two babies together. In addition to this, they had enough strength and patience to give me love and support to push the limits, as well as patience for my frayed temper and nervousness stemming from being overtired while building a business. That still did not take me away from taking part in my daughters' upbringing and jumping out of bed at night with their every cry and bringing them to Ivana so that she can get some rest as well. I am grateful for my two daughters whose cognitive empathy is like a blessing from God. I am grateful for my wife's fierceness that gives us mental stability and makes us realize what a happy family we are, not for what we have achieved, but for realizing that the center of happiness lies in our mutual love, good health and spirit.

I am also grateful to my parents who pushed me into playing basketball and taking that endeavor across the pond as that definitely set the direction for the rest of my life. I guess that the fanatic determination to survive and excel at anything and everything that I carry with me comes from them.

So… the Engineers were born. Remember these four names: Aleksandar Zivkovic, Goran Silic, Mladen Jovic, Dragan Drazic. When I think of these four guys, I keep thinking of the words "the Four Horsemen of the Apocalypse". There is nothing that they and the apocalypse have in common, other than when I run the business to the apocalypse and back, they ride with me no matter what. Maybe if it hadn't been for them, I would have thought of quitting this fight at times. Back to those times of being young and inexperienced (stupid): I thought once you lift your business off the ground, everything is smooth in going forward… ha ha ha ha ha! It's never easy, just the level of the game increases, but you either take that as reality and live with it like it's nothing or you go get yourself an eight-to-four job. I would not be wrong if I said that the reason for this book, the very 12-milestone methodology, the Ivan Agency and Engineers London is the collective experience of the five of us. The only thing is, as they took it upon themselves to replace and multiply my effort, only better, I was the only one with some extra time to put this experience into writing.

INTRODUCTION1

Concepting – a general notion or idea; a conception. An idea of something formed by mentally combining all its characteristics or particulars; a construct.

Digital Product Idea – a result of the thinking process which lays the foundation in one's field of knowledge and experience and results in mental visualization of a new product or an improvement to an existing one.

The majority of products fail. They fail for two reasons: one is the very product, while the other is the business that operates it. What this book deals with is making sure the product is not the reason for business failure. This trend is present not only in startups but also in SMEs and enterprises. It is important to grasp this: there is a business and there is a product, in which case the product is a business tool. Let's imagine a race track for a moment and think about a car and a driver in this analogy: the car is the product and the driver is the founder; the driver (founder) employs the best of his/her skills, knowledge and experience to operate the car (product) in order to get from point A to point B (from investment to profitability) in the most efficient manner (the most efficient utilization of resources) so as to cross the finishing line as a handful of the best (successfully goes through the technology adoption lifecycle and crosses the chasm1; if you are not familiar with it – in the simplest terms, make the business sustainable).

---

[1] Crossing the Chasm: Marketing and Selling High-Tech Products to Mainstream Customers or simply Crossing the Chasm is a marketing book by Geoffrey A. Moore.

If the product is what it needs to be and it performs, it is only up to the business to make it a success. Both the product and the business must be in sync at all times.

"Before light there was darkness" and before business there was product, whereas before product there was idea. The transformation of that idea into a digital product and a synchronized coexistence of the product and the idea is the process that can destine the business to success or failure.

One of the primary reasons for the aforementioned failure is the lack of proper product development (concepting, as I prefer to call it). In this case, the product may not fail early in the process, but it will in the early stages of its life-cycle because of the way it had been concepted. There is a strong bond between this and how the product was built, but that is a different topic that I will briefly address at the end of the book.

Failure may occur as early as product design stage, it can be as harmful as failure during software development, and as costly as the scenario in which a defective product reaches the customers. The best moment for a product to fail and for you to be happy about it is during concepting when the least effort and the smallest amount of resources are invested in the product and when everything that comes after can be validated, especially the design, the build, and the road to the market.

This book is about the concepting of digital products and even though the entire process can amount to ten rules, there is so much more to it —which is the very reason this book was written. I have concepted and built over two hundred products with my core team. This book is the result of more than a decade of hands-on experience and during that time I witnessed many successes, but even more failures. This book is focused on my 12-milestone methodology for digital product concepting and it offers the reader the means to sustain great inspirations to avoid hidden and inevitable risks of failure. I tried to choose the adequate verb that would portray exactly how great inspirations need to be managed, since, even though they are the primary driver of a new business, they also put that future business at risk. At times, you will need to sustain your great inspirations, whereas, at times, you will have to restrain them.

Rule 1
Do not start creating a digital product with a design nor with a development of designs.

Rule 2
Specify what is to be developed and cover all crucial details prior to the development.

Rule 3
Start off by developing an MVP.

Rule 4
Do not leave any crucial details to interpretation.

Rule 5
Know what you are developing and who you are developing it for.

Rule 6
Know why you are developing each of the features and what the value of each feature is to the future user/customer.

Rule 7
Document everything.

Rule 8

Prepare the effort estimates that are based on the project documentation.

Rule 9

Collect and analyze data.

Rule 10

Plan a product roadmap based on the collected and analyzed data.

A digital product (in further text – product) refers to a consumer-facing product that is in the form of Mobile App, Web App, Desktop/Platform/Embedded App, or a combination of any of these. For example, Instagram is a product that is in the form of both Mobile and Web apps, where the dominant product is the Mobile app.

While the product can be a tool, a business solution, a social network, a game, and so on, it also refers to the implementation of any trendy topics/terms such as AR, VR, AI, ML, Wearable, IoT, OTT, blockchain and similar.

LIFE EXPERIENCES INFLUENCE OUR WORK CREATIONS

Let's focus on startups for a bit. Looking at startup founders as individuals and their life stories, I have distinguished four situations that spark the creation of new digital products from an individual perspective.

Situation 1: Digital products built on personal lifestyle needs

Let's say your regular day starts off by drinking coffee at one of your favorite coffee shops; you always use loyalty cards and enjoy getting free coffee every now and then even though it does not influence your budget. Long story short, you decide to build a loyalty card app for coffee shops and start selling locally to the coffee shop owners you already know; with a number of magical occurrences, things go viral and you got yourself a solid business.

I cannot say this is an exact story replica of how AirBnb Started, but I would classify it under the same category.

These situations are so rare that I doubt there is even a one percent success rate, but it sounds great, doesn't it? The main problem here is that you are most probably not utilizing your knowledge, experience and network, but rather going on a hunch without any market research, proof of concept, evidence of a business need and just think of how great that would be from your perspective. I've seen so many startups fail because they thought building something they found "awesome" would be a winning business. To elaborate further, I will move onto the second situation.

Situation 2: Digital products built on personal, yet professional business needs

Let's say you are an accountant and you are recognizing the one thing none of the accounting softwares out there provide; you realize the opportunity for a software that would be so useful that an accountant would be a total amateur not to purchase it; you have it built and start selling through your networks and it just goes through the roof.

Slack began as an internal tool born out of personal, yet professional, necessity. Slack founder, Stewart Butterfield, explains that the company knew exactly how people were using Slack long before making it public to customers. Very importantly, they were lead by the thought they should teach users why they need their product. You can do that only if you are building a business in the environment and industry you are comfortable in.

The key difference between the first and second category is exactly that - you are building a business in the environment and industry you are comfortable in. You have the knowledge of the industry and know how things work, you know what the software must do based on your experience, you know that no one else has done it as you are using accounting apps all the time and exploring new ones as you want to improve your business. You are simply realizing an opportunity based on tangible evidence and acting within your comfort zone. While in the first example with the coffee shops, drinking coffee is just your lifestyle and you are not owning a chain of coffee shops nor anything similar, the accountant example is strictly your profession and most definitely not your lifestyle.

Slack began as an internal tool born out of personal, yet professional, necessity. The Slack founder, Stewart Butterfield, explains that the company knew exactly how people were using Slack long before making it public to customers. More importantly, they were lead by the thought they should teach users why they need their product. You can do that only if you are building a business in the environment and industry you are comfortable in.

The key difference between the first and the second category is exactly that – you are building a business in the environment and the industry you are comfortable in. You have the knowledge of the industry and know how things work, you know what the software must do based on your experience, you know that no one else has done it as you use accounting apps all the time and explore the new ones because you want to improve your business. You are simply realizing an opportunity based on tangible evidence and acting within your comfort zone. While in the first example with the coffee shops, drinking coffee is just your lifestyle and you don't own a chain of coffee shops or anything similar, the accountant example is strictly your profession and most definitely not your lifestyle.

Situation 3: Digital products built on lifestyle needs, where your lifestyle is your profession

Let's say you are a professional DJ; you build a DJ mixer app based on your clearly recognizable need for one.

Same as our friend the accountant, you have the knowledge, you have the experience, you have the network, but most importantly, you are living that life. An accountant is not an accountant when clubbing or socializing or jogging, since accounting cannot be a lifestyle, however, a DJ is always a DJ and expresses that at all times as being a DJ is simply a lifestyle.

When Garrick Barr left his coaching position with Phoenix Suns in 2004, he permanently changed the way basketball coaches, baseball coaches and general managers do their jobs. He founded Synergy, a

tech company that become the leader in basketball and baseball sports industry when it comes to providing data, analytics and tools for coaches and general managers enabling them to evaluate players, create scouting reports and build game plans.

Coach is a coach, that's the way of life, and so is basketball!

Situation 4: Digital products built on a foundation of work-life balance

If you can balance your work and your life so that your work is part of your life and your life experiences positively influence your work and vice versa, then whatever digital product, born out of your experiences, will place you in a position where your personal lifestyle needs do include your professional business needs and you fall into a category where you are still not that DJ but you can still have that kind of balance. I believe this is where the most startup founders should fit in.

Let's say you are a travel agent and you keep stressing about negative feedback from the vacation packages you sold and a lack of relative information you would use to form better packages; your work is suffering and you are transferring that stress onto your family; your work-life imbalance is clogging your thoughts and you are forcing yourself into eating, drinking, but rarely, training more; all of a sudden you manage to simplify things and look at them from a different perspective trying to find an innovative solution rather than working harder to resolve something that cannot be resolved with more power but with a different perspective – smarter work; you come up with an idea for an app where your clients can share their vacation expectations and previous travel experiences; your AI-enabled app is then able to give advice on travel packages that best suit your clients, and not only do you win your clients over but you also automate a lot of your daily work; clients start liking the app you brought to life, they start enjoying working with you more, and they spread the word to all their friends who share the same passion for traveling; your business reaches the heights that were unexpected just half a year ago; you are happy, your stress level is down, everything is great!

The point is – you managed to balance out your life and work so that work is not something influencing your life negatively, but complementing it with positivity and you live a life where work is part of it in the same way as play, training, socializing, traveling or anything else is.

When Adam Lowe and Shib Hussain, two marketing storytelling geniuses, decided to take control of their work-life balance, they never thought official feedback from Apple would be "Perhaps the most ambitious interactive narrative platform we've seen so far". The real-life fiction product they envisioned, the high quality product they got built, and the timely and well-thought entrepreneurial decisions they made put them on a good path to make this work-life balance a reality. It was a true pleasure taking part in the early days of their UNRD story.

.

DIVERSE VALUE OF DIGITAL TRANSFORMATION

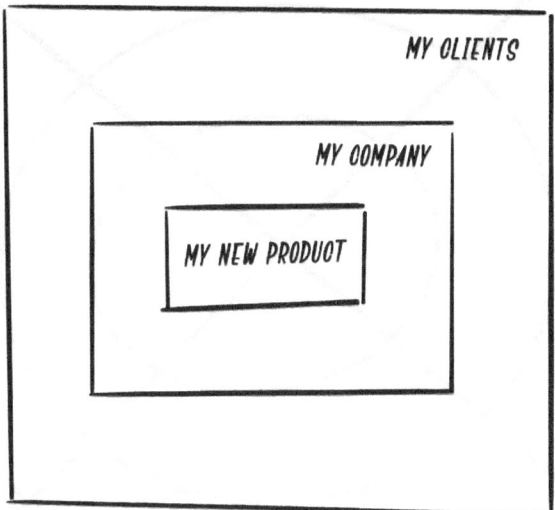

I must refer to non-startups as well, as this entire story is agnostic to the type, scale or success of a business.

Digital Transformation is the novel use of digital technology to solve traditional problems. It represents the integration of digital technology into all areas of a business, fundamentally changing how you operate and deliver value to customers. It's also a cultural change that requires organizations to continually challenge the way they operate, to experiment with said areas and get comfortable with failure.

A new innovative product can enhance a business both externally and internally. The external enhancement is reflected in a product that is client-facing, while the internal enhancement is reflected in a product that improves and optimizes the internal business processes.

Very often does a product enhance a business both externally and internally. Thanks to a digital agency based in central London, MadeByChapter[2], which consists of an established team of creative individuals with a combined passion for branding, marketing and technology, I had a fantastic opportunity to work alongside them with The Economist-owned TVC Group, a content agency that offers expertise across media and influencer relations, social, digital and production. Years ago, they became true innovation leaders in their field by creating The Digital News Agency (DNA)[3], an award-winning proprietary content-hosting solution providing tens of thousands of global broadcasters and journalists with access to a variety of multimedia content from the latest brand-led stories and campaigns. Time passed and the way the solution was utilized internally and

---

[2] https://www.madebychapter.com/

[3] https://digitalnewsagency.com/

externally had to change and adapt. It simply had to go through a new iteration of upgrades to avoid becoming obsolete.

While the goal for the new upgraded version was to enhance value provided to the end-users (journalists and broadcasters), we simply had to analyze how that value is achieved in order to enhance it. I spent some time interviewing key solution consumers and realized the solution lay in making internal teams who manage the dysfunctional and out-of-sync content, while the utilization of the solution is consuming too much of their time. That obviously must cause a negative effect to the end-users as it affects the quality of the content and may have other side effects. Regardless, the capable TVC team found their way around it in order to provide the best value for the client, but the fact remains that they used to spend too much of their time and effort on something that should have been fluent.

We have used the 12-milestone methodology to reinvent The Digital News Agency. When the solution was delivered based on the project elaborate, the effects on the content editor, the content manager, the client services, and the sales teams were profound. An emission of positivity that these effects had, the software architecture that cut hosting expenses in half, together with an enhanced product for the end-users —it all made this project a true example of a successful digital transformation.

12-MILESTONE METHODOLOGY FOR DIGITAL PRODUCT CONCEPTING

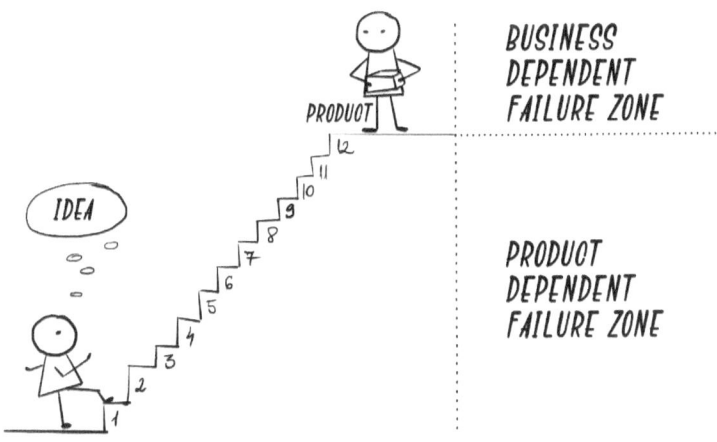

The 12-milestone methodology is based on the principles of Lean Startup, Design Thinking, Agile Project Management and Technology Adoption Life Cycle and can be applied alongside the listed methodologies.

The 12-milestone methodology is composed of a predefined list of actions or a choice of actions that define how an idea is led from a thought to a fully built product.

The methodology has a core purpose to take an idea by hand, in any stage, shape or form, and transform it into a blueprint of a future product. The methodology renders the possibility of failing to deliver the digital product obsolete, it assures the project delivery within the estimated time and cost, and ensures that the digital product is not the reason for a business's failure (the most common scenario that we want to avoid and the very reason for this book).

Furthermore, the methodology leads the business owner to valid assumptions and positive validations for the investment in the new venture.

Simplifying things often gives a different perspective, and clearing out all the clutter brings out purity. Many complex systems fail when the basics are left neglected. "Back to basics" may be a cliché, but it's very often the solution, too. Staying aware of the basics of your product, of your business, and of yourself, will help you keep following the compass at all times.

During the writing of this book, I was working with Jenny Connick, the founder of Talentino Careers[4], on the digital transformation of one of their prime products "It's in the Box!". "It's in the Box!" is a career coaching program with the purpose of enabling children between 7

---

[4] http://www.talentinocareers.co.uk/

and 13 years old in the UK education curriculum to make thoughtful career decisions by exploring options, creating career development plans, engaging with employers and developing employability skills. The goal of my engagement was to concept a digital product based on the physical one that will put Talentino Careers in a favorable position for exponential growth. The end result of this endeavor was a digital product concept that Jenny truly loved, as, together with my team, I managed to digitize a product without losing its integral value. At the same time, my team produced valid effort estimates for the delivery of the product that she could incorporate into her business plan and go after an investment.

USE CASE APP: MeetMe@

While documenting the 12-milestone methodology, I simply had to back it up with a real-world-use case. We had created a concept for a simple app named MeetMe@ for that reason.

Running across London from one meeting to another, I tend to avoid offices and meet my clients and prospects at various locations across the city – I find it more inspiring, motivational and comfortable for casual, yet serious discussions. To make it real and worthwhile, MeetMe@ was envisioned as an elegant new take on navigating yourself or a group to a meeting point.

MeetMe@ is a location-based app, which overcomes the burden of explaining to someone where to meet. Once you invite your contacts to a meeting point, you are able to see their whereabouts on the map until they reach the destination. If you have been invited, you also have the whereabouts of all the people in the group until they reach the destination.

To make it even more realistic, we had also placed focus on safety. For that reason, this app does not require you to register, but rather asks for your nickname and photo in order for others in the group to identify you with ease. You can always leave and rejoin the process of meeting with a group. The app informs all participants as soon as someone arrives at the location.

The benefits of this app are twofold. First of all, the MeetMe@ elaborate is a great add-on value to this book, and together with the app build, it provides compelling evidence of my 12-milestone methodology. Additionally, not only is the app a useful tool for running across London, but it also gives a powerful demonstration of the leads prior to meeting them for the first time in person.

MILESTONE 1 – GET PERSONAL WITH YOUR PRODUCT IDEA AND BE SURE YOU LOVE IT

My primary goal is to explain how to take that idea of yours and develop it into a fully blown digital product – a product that you can base your business on and a product that you can rely on. Let's focus on the first step that seems so small and insignificant, yet it is the first of many and the most important one.

Go ahead and write down your idea in one precise sentence, like a soldier. This is very important – you have to be able to write it down in one sentence, leave all the decorations out – literally, what the hell are you going to build?! Just like when someone cannot grasp what you're talking about and you yell it out to them so straightforwardly that they must understand, if they have any sanity left in them. That tends to be very difficult – your idea is always in a number of thoughts, it is all over the place. It is very obvious what it is, but condensing that into one sentence is very difficult. Write it down, spend a full day on it and then go to bed, go to sleep, go to the gym, just leave it. Don't think about it at all. Come back to it tomorrow.

How do you feel about that idea, about that sentence, today? Do you feel inspired or are you thinking – who the hell wrote this and it's definitely not me!? Repeat the process until you feel good about what you wrote down. Then leave it for a week and question it once again. Once you feel good about the idea, test it out – tell your friends, family, associates, colleagues, tell them that one sentence and note their reaction. It is crucial that you do! Don't take that feedback for granted, not because you should listen to everyone's feedback, but think about why that person is relevant and to which extent and decide how to take that feedback. Many of the world's best digital products were built without listening to feedback. You will know if you're nailing it, and you will certainly know if you're not. If you aren't – restart! If you are, do you love it?

As you will be modifying that idea along the way, try to base the changes of your opinion on something that you can hold on to. Keep a written record of your decisions. One needs that solid ground in order to stop questioning themselves and their idea: if you provide yourself with evidence of why you made a certain decision, you will feel much more confident about it.

One of my clients, a London-based GDPR in Schools Limited, bases their business on a product for comprehensive GDPR monitoring and management in schools. With a new GDPR legislation in the EU since May 2018, the legal entities that could get into serious trouble are schools, for managing and processing highly sensitive children's personal data. The schools' responsibility burden is massive. Getting fined for a data privacy-related mistake while prioritizing children over profits for the children's well-being would be a massive disaster. GDPRiS is a monster project with tons of features. Putting them in one sentence seems impossible. For example: "GDPRiS is a highly secure, cloud-based tool designed to reflect existing processes and the way schools work, whilst pro-actively prompting them to meet and exceed the new General Data Protection Regulations. The best of the best is combined in GDPRiS, it documents data flows, mapping and auditing of all personal data, and prompts the use of SAQs. It will guide all school staff to a new level of data protection understanding."[5] However, saying GDPRiS is a comprehensive GDPR monitoring and management solution for schools sums it up in one sentence. While the meaning of that one sentence does not have to be meaningful to wide audiences, it must be meaningful to your target audiences. Furthermore, not only is it impossible to explain your product in one sentence while listing all of its features, but it is wrong and it leads nowhere.

---

[5] Quote from GDPRiS Web site https://www.gdpr.school/

MILESTONE 2 — DEFINE TARGET AUDIENCES AND RECOGNIZE THE OBVIOUS SEGMENTATIONS WITHIN

A target audience is a particular group at which a product is aimed. There can be a number of target audiences for a digital product. Target audiences can be defined once a product vision and a core purpose are defined. Of course you will have an idea of your target audience when your idea is born, but here I'm talking about the definition of the target audience.

Action 1: Assume and elaborate a target audience.

The concepting of digital products must start with assumptions. That is the very reason each of these 12 milestones is planned in a particular order so that one thing leads to another. At times, digital products are born out of necessity and already have dedicated clients awaiting, but most of the time that is not the case.

Other than you, naturally, who may want to use your product? You obviously realize a need for it; still, it is crucial to define who will want to use it. Start from yourself. In order to realize various target audiences, you need to define various use cases. Every digital product can be used in various ways for various needs.

Let's take a banal case and generalize it even further just to prove the point – iWatch. Its obvious use cases are for someone to check the time, to track their physical activity, to react to notifications effortlessly, or to answer a call. Therefore, target audiences may include someone who uses a watch for nothing more than checking what time it is, but does so using a trendy gadget, and someone who is a recreational athlete or even a professional athlete, and someone who is working in a fast-paced environment, is highly dependent on their mobile phone, but has no time to keep picking up the phone.

Action 2: If you are the key actor within your target audience (and you will be in one way or another), recognize who you are in your story and extract new target audiences.

Obviously, there are many possibilities there. Try to find as many different scenarios that you haven't thought of originally. Never concept a product only around your personal needs – you may end up being the only user! Do some research by interviewing your friends, family, and colleagues – how would they feel about using this product in such situations? Interested? Not at all interested? Confused? Doubtful? Do not ask for their opinion on whether they think the business could work, ask them if they would use the product. That's very important to differentiate.

Additionally, try expanding that circle by creating a simple online questionnaire and conducting simple research in a community available to you through social or business networks. You need to explain to some extent what you want to do, but still, without revealing too much at this stage. You need to lead them into a position in which you want them to be. That questionnaire would need to have a few different scenarios covered, so create a few questionnaires that suit the needs of the potential target audience you somewhat identified. Realize that you are already setting up the foundation for your future marketing efforts for the product this early in the process.

This approach leads not only to getting feedback about the idea, but most importantly, it leads towards recognizing obvious target audiences and realistic use cases. After all, you do not even have to conduct that questionnaire, you'll know if you need to or not by your own intuition.

Action 3: Define Who will use your product, How/When and Why.

Make sure you can answer the following questions:

1. Who will use my product?

2. How and when will they use my product?

3. Why would they use my product?

Create a simple table with three columns: Who, How/When, Why. It is very important to note this – never say everyone! Identify who those people are, describe them! Identify as many obvious target audiences as possible. You can go as deep as identifying buyer personas, but I do not consider that to be absolutely necessary.

Action 4: Recognize the obvious segmentation within each of the Target Audiences.

By definition, market segmentation is the process of dividing a market of potential customers into groups, or segments, based on different characteristics. The segments created are composed of consumers who will respond similarly to marketing strategies and who share traits such as similar interests, needs, or locations.

How to recognize segmentation within a Target Audience? Let's say this sentence defines our product: An app for anonymous and instant location-sharing with a goal to meet at a desired location[6].

---

[6] Use case app built for this book: MeetMe@ - Live meeting points; look it up at App and Play Stores.

Obviously, a logical target audience may be tourists.

Who the tourists may be:

• Group of friends/family exploring a city or countryside (Tourists, yet friends/family who travel)
• Tourist guide leading a random group of people (Tourists, yet Travel agency or a Travel guide)
• Teacher leading a group of students (Tourists, yet Ed-tech)

This gives us obvious segmentation within the tourists target audience:

• Travelers (Friends/Families)
• Travel agencies
• Travel guides
• Teachers

Action 5: Elaborate the main premises of Milestone 2.

Requirements for the vision of the MVP version: I can clearly identify my MVP – the minimum that my product must be in order to serve the core business purpose. If I do not know that, I will keep getting ideas while developing my product. As I develop the product and get ideas, I will be easily drawn to changing the scope and, therefore, the delivery date and, certainly, the cost. As I change the delivery date, I obviously increase my expenses and I cannot plan the next steps. I must be aware of the fact that building a product is just the beginning – the product needs to get users sooner or later, so how do you approach those users?

Who do you recognize as the major target audience: Not knowing who my users are, and simply assuming they are just like me, I am being ignorant of who will use the product and how. If I know who and how and why, I will be able to adapt the product so that its MVP can serve the vast majority of my target audience.

Start planning how to approach the target audience: By knowing my target audience, I will know how to market the product. I will know who I need to reach, where to direct my marketing, which businesses to approach and how to present my product to them. I will be able to think about my first users (innovators), my early adopters, my early majority and my late majority. I can start thinking about my business and how to make a business where my product is its driving power.

Start thinking of the MVP vs the next phases of development against the Target Audience layout: I will spend only what I must spend to release the product. I will be able to plan the delivery of my next features based on how my marketing plan works, how successful my reach is to my target audience. If the features that are directed towards one target group are working and aren't towards others, I will direct my efforts towards the Target audience that works, and not spend time and money on building a product and a marketing plan towards the audiences that have no affection for my product. The metrics that my future product collects will have a major influence here, but it is not time to bring them into play yet. The metrics represent the analyzed data collected from digital product consumption that signify trends in product and product-feature consumption.

"If you build it, they will come" – "Field of Dreams", a movie from 1989, starring Kevin Costner, portrays a delusion of pursuing your vision as if the outcome will always be positive. This is probably the worst situation a startup founder can be in, yet the majority of entrepreneurs find themselves in this situation. That's perfectly fine if you are Dr Dre and your product is Beats, otherwise do not fool yourself…

A few years ago, I was working with this fantastic entrepreneur – very successful, very result-driven – on a mobile app that collects all the social feeds in one place so that a social follower does not have to open ten different apps to consume all the content but rather have a central place for it all. It did seem like a great idea, and maybe it still is. This was a software development effort where my Engineers put mind-blowing effort into delivering an update to the app for Bob Geldof's Band Aid 30 remake of "Do They Know It's Christmas?" in just a few days. Ten developers and designers literally did not sleep for three days straight. Bob Geldof recorded it to raise funds for the Ebola crisis in western Africa. The app was used as a means of donating funds during that one day and thanks to a single tweet from One Direction, fifty thousand signups to the app occurred in just one hour. The song was knocked off the top of the U.K. singles chart after only a week. The same happened to the app metrics. That is completely fine for the song, but not as much for the app. The main point here was that the app had a very precise, very defined, very obvious target audience for that one day or one week. However, as soon as that target audience dissolved, there was no defined target audience and the metrics of the app became disturbing.

The app performed perfectly and therefore the goal of making sure the app was not the cause of business failure was accomplished, which is all a software development agency can accomplish when being hired to deliver per specification. Many fail at that as well, so I will revert to this topic towards the end of the book. However, the business failed – it failed on the second milestone of the 12-milestone methodology, so the very reason I described this situation is for you to understand how far you can go with your digital product and yet fail due to something you had to have defined in the first week of your future digital product endeavor.

Still, if you look even further back, milestone one is based on questioning your idea. Ten years ago, in distant 2009, Gary Vaynerchuk explained in his book Crush It! the following: each social media platform is specific and so your content must be adherent to each one. That is not due to the platform itself but rather to the kind of users of each platform. Maybe that would have been sufficient evidence that could have invalidated the idea of this app.

As elaborated earlier in milestone two – make sure you are not your only target audience. When you look at this idea from a business perspective, it makes sense since your business is required to be on a number of social networks. However, that is only because your business needs to be exposed to various target audiences, not because you want to reach the same person on five different social or business networks.

MILESTONE 3 — GENERATE MONETIZATION POTENTIAL FOR YOUR DIGITAL PRODUCT BY DEFINING THE MAIN VALUE PROPOSITIONS

We produced greater leverage for success by defining target audiences due to the fact that we recognized a greater, yet defined market, for the new product. What that means is — if we totally fail in regard to some target audiences, we still have the market.

Does that sound as though we would have to build the product to suit a greater number of audiences? It does, in some way, but that is a flawed assumption. I'll explain why that is through three key actions of the Main Value Proposition milestone of my 12-milestone process.

Main Value Propositionsare values your product will provide to your end-users (target audiences). They are the reason why your end-users will use your product and are also the foundation of your future business. If this product provides value to someone, there are ways to monetize it.

Action 1: Generalize Target Audiences into obvious groups

The goal here is to provide a common value to all Target Audiences. If we generalize target audiences into smaller groups, it is easier to recognize shared common values.

This directly refers to the first milestone and the importance of defining the core of the product — if the core is defined properly, it will be easier and more feasible to define values for all Target Audiences.

Let's revert to our use case app for the book (MeetMe@). Target audiences for the MeetMe@ app are: groups of friends with an active social life, tourists and travelers, recreational athletes and entrepreneurs.

We can generalize these into two groups of users:

1. Social users
2. Business users

These two groups are not set in stone for every product – my intention is to lead you to think in the direction that will make you recognize obvious generalized groups for your own product.

We always have to keep target audiences in mind: through the aforementioned process, we are not neglecting them, we are just generalizing them for higher purposes.

This already signifies a monetization potential through Business users or advanced Social user features.

Please note the logical advancement in the process. If we hadn't defined the core of the product in Milestone 1, we could not have defined Target audiences in Milestone 2. If we hadn't defined Target audiences in Milestone 2, we could not have defined the Main value propositions in Milestone 3. Now that we know who our users will be and what the value we can provide to them is, we can think about how we can monetize this idea.

Action 2: Define the Primary and Secondary Main Value Propositions for each Target Audience group

The primary Main Value Propositions are values that are direct and obvious values that can be further broken down into more detailed values.

The secondary Main Value Propositions are derived from the primary Main Value Propositions. This does not mean they have a lower value than the Primary ones, but rather that they are an extension of the Primary ones.

Let's lay down this information in the following format by taking the MeetMe@ use case app as a reference, in which Social and Business would be the groups you defined in the previous step. To refresh your memory, MeetMe@ is an app for anonymous and instant location-sharing between a group of people with a common goal to meet at a desired location. I will list only a few values in order to elaborate this step.

Value	Primary	Secondary	Social	Business
Value of knowing the invitees will arrive at the meeting destination	X		X	X
Value of knowing the whereabouts of the group that has a common target to meet at the destination	X		X	X
Anonymous location-sharing amongst a group of people who aren't necessarily associated with each other	X		X	X
Allows for planning of an activity in relation to an early arrival of the invitees to the destination		X	X	X

Reduces risks of someone in the group getting lost when at an unfamiliar location & improves the safety of the group		x	x	x

Action 3: Conclude if the values are common across all groups

Based on the table above, it is obvious that both groups share the same values.

It would be good to elaborate at least one of these values in order to make it clear. Let's take the following one: "Reduces risks of someone in the group getting lost when at an unfamiliar location & improves the safety of the group."

A group of colleagues is on a business trip to a foreign location. Someone may get drunk, someone may get robbed, someone may get lost, someone might want to spend their free time outside the group… It is of high importance to meet at a desired location at a desired time, as it is essential for business success. Same goes for casual/social travels. This is obviously a separate group and has a separate meaning, but the value stays the same.

What we can conclude with certainty now is that both Social and Business audiences have the same Main Value Propositions. We clearly identified both groups and we identified the values, now we can proceed to see how we can monetize this product.

Target audience groups being split into social and business categories is a very common scenario and a proven model. Look at Instagram for example, where a regular (social) user has neither interest in promoting posts nor does he/she have an option to do so, while a user with a business account is given that option. Promoting a post gives the user business value and they spend money based on that value proposition.

MILESTONE 4 — PRICING STRATEGY AND REVENUE STREAMS

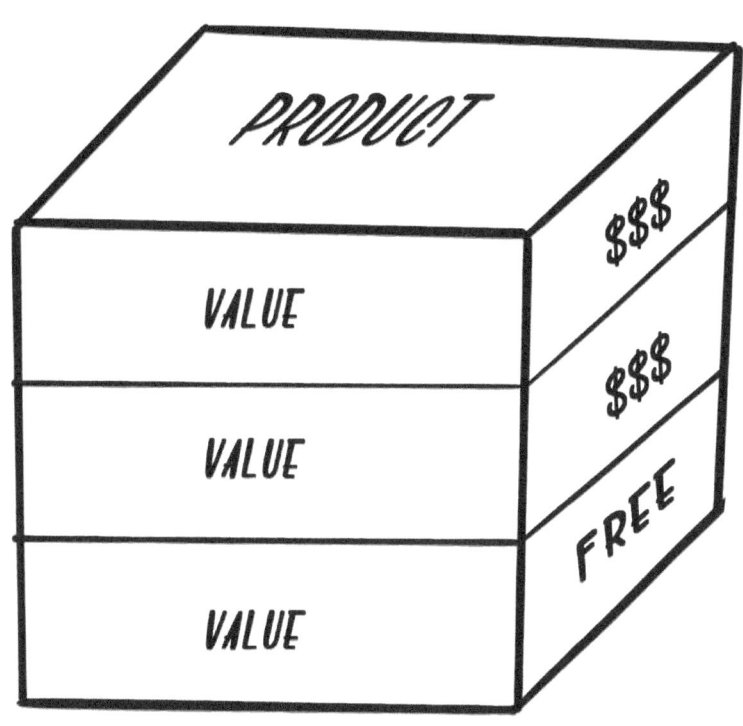

Talking about product monetization this early in the process sounds questionable. The reason for this is very simple — monetization of the product influences the features of the product. If you've settled on how to monetize the product at the very beginning, your focus while concepting will be on monetization and it will influence the product features.

Action 1: Determine if the product is freemium or premium

Freemium is a pricing strategy in which a product or a service is provided free of charge, but additional features, services, or virtual or physical goods are charged. "Freemium" is a blending of the words "free" and "premium". The idea is to offer your basic service for free, acquire a lot of customers very efficiently through various marketing means, mostly social, and then offer premium-priced value-added services or an enhanced version to your customer base.

On the other hand, a premium product has to be purchased or subscribed to in order to be used. The most that is given to users is a demo which obviously must demonstrate the software's Main Value Propositions.

When it comes to MeetMe@ — this app is a social tool. It has a number of mechanisms that can increase the usage of the app considerably. It is enough to reach one user who will invite another ten for a meeting, meaning one customer acquires another ten, while there is no barrier to entry due to a simplistic Web version that allows for the usage of the product without installing the app.

Therefore, it can be concluded that the MeetMe@ app falls under the category of the Freemium model.

Action 2: Identify the free features (if any)

Identification of the free features should be a no-brainer at this point. Simply make a linear bulleted list of these items.

Action 3: Decide if the MVP should offer premium features

There are a few factors on which this decision depends. These factors are your business decisions which are not discussed in my 12-milestone process. However, I feel that this action is needed at this point and therefore will provide some guidelines. These decisions should be made once the entire 12-milestone process is completed as the estimates (Milestone 11) will elaborate timelines and the required funding.

1. **Funding:** First you need to ask yourself, how much fuel do you have to play this game?

2. **Timeline:** If you decide to release the free features, it will most probably not be for another three months before you release the paid features. Why three months? So that you have enough time to collect and analyze the data that will influence your premium features release plan.

3. **User acquisition:** Can you afford acquiring the users and not monetizing the features for three months, or six even? Have you already started acquiring users prior to the MVP release? What happens if it takes you a year to start monetizing the features?

4. **Data:** Your product must have a built-in means of collecting data and providing metrics. Analyzing the metrics is of crucial importance for your future product.

Action 4: Identify the premium features (if any)

At this stage, you should decide whether your MVP will be released with the Freemium or the Premium pricing strategy.

Expand the list you created for the free features by cross-referencing free and paid features:

Feature	Free	Paid
Feature 1	X	X
Feature 2	X	X
Feature 3		X

Way too many times have I heard "We just need lots of users and we'll see how we'll make money". Certainly, many aspects of the future product will transform into something different over time. It's the same with monetization. Take Twitter, for example: they had no monetization plan in sight for years and are still struggling. Twitter being a phenomenon, don't start from an assumption that your digital product will be one as well, as there aren't many Twitters around the world.

MILESTONE 5 — DO NOT SPOIL YOUR IDEA WHEN SKETCHING A NEW DIGITAL PRODUCT

The concept of a digital product, whether it is an app, a website, an IoT product or anything else, can be sketched whenever. However, sketching is left for the 5th step in the digital product concepting endeavor, it will be produced with much more quality and it will require much less effort.

I know, it is intriguing to sketch ideas straight away, so give it a try. You will see how many questions and concerns will arise. Go mad over the sketches, do not worry, do not question them, just sketch it all out, whatever is in your mind. Once you feel empty, leave sketching, go do something totally different and keep your thoughts away from the product.

When you return, take your product through Milestones 1 through 4 of my 12-milestone digital product concepting and innovation methodology, and then return to sketching. 95% of everything will be so clear that the very process will be much less troublesome, you will have questions answered and resolutions already found.

Most importantly, you will find purity in your idea, you will keep the idea whole and intact, only improved, in contrast to a very high probability of getting so excited about the idea that you may decorate it so much and go to extremes that put such a heavy coat over it that the very idea cannot be recognized anymore — exactly what Milestones 1 through 4 make you do, they put all the focus on the initial idea, on the initial spark of creativity and geniosity.

You may wonder, why sketch at this point, why not wireframe digitally? For the very reason that things can be done so much faster by hand, on a piece of paper — on that note, a tablet and a digital pen will do just as fine as the old school tools. I just kind of like those basics, it makes it feel more like a garage startup that will become a unicorn. It simply provides inspiration. It makes you more connected to the product, to the nature of it. It will attract some good karma…

After fifteen years of working for clients and only finding time to produce some smaller fun products for my own satisfaction[7], circumstances collided in such a way that I was heavily invested in my first major product while writing this book. It's been years since I've dedicated sixteen to eighteen hours per day to working, and while my daughters lack my presence and attention, I believe I am teaching them about dedication and passion as I talk to them about what I work on and I try to teach them about life using my everyday circumstances. Anyway, this is not a story about entrepreneurial principles and life, there are enough great entrepreneurs speaking about it (and a few abusing the momentum, as is the case with everything in today's world). The reason I had to mention this is directly related to the principles of the 12-milestone methodology which focuses on goal-oriented dedication to work and life.

---

[7] https://https://engineers.london/ This is my and my team's playground! We love producing mobile games and digital products that entertain and educate. We enjoy being annoyed while trying to beat our own creations!

MILESTONE 6 — INCREMENTALLY IMPROVE THE CONCEPT

Get the best out of an idea in the moment when all creativity is at its maximum. This is the point in time when everything can still be revised until every stakeholder is satisfied, while invested time and money are at their minimum. Nothing has gone too far yet, it has only gotten to the point where revisions are time and cost-effective. The revisions are cost-effective as you are still on a piece of paper and the only investment is your time or the time of someone who you paid to sketch your idea. Imagine how that compares to changing a product that is already in development.

The key deliverables are: a rough sketch of a fully blown product based on the premises from the 1st milestone, further expansion of the idea and the features laid out in milestones 2 through 5 (to the level of acceptable effort and imagination). This is the moment where you can play to the maximum and visualize everything the product can be. Once you have that, it will be easy to pick what the true MVP of the future digital product is.

Speaking of that product of mine, there were about ten different features that were initially all recognized as mandatory for the MVP. We managed to iteratively simplify the product down to two core features, since it turned out that the other eight were simply a different angle of looking at the same thing. The amount of future effort in executing and maintaining that product was decreased by sixty percent! Imagine if your MVP cost $40k instead of $100k because you spent a few days more with a piece of paper?! That also brings me to another conclusion which is a common cooperation obstacle in this industry. How much does that effort cost (the concepting effort)? Can it be measured in a number of days or in the value that it produces? The same should be with your future product – craft a product that will produce value! I will reiterate that a few times – if a product produces value to someone, then there is a reason for someone to use it and there is a reason for someone to pay for it.

MILESTONE 7 — REALIZE YOUR DELIVERY PHASES AND DELIVERY PHASE INFLUENCES

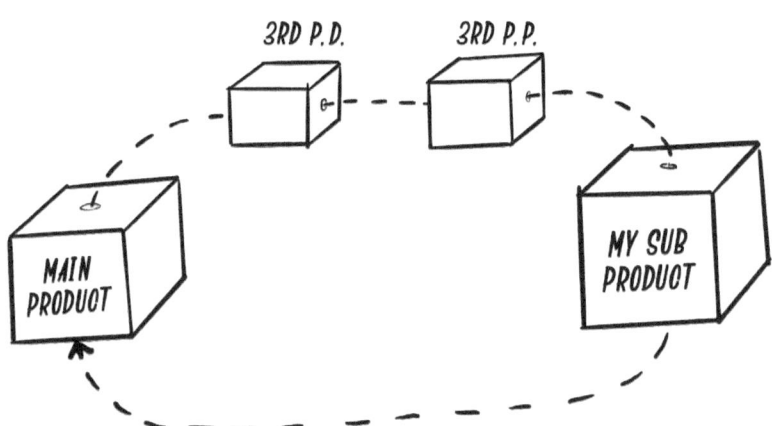

PRODUCT ECOSYSTEM

It is time to decide what your Minimum Viable Product features are, in other words, the minimum that your product must have in order to serve the core business purpose. Everything less than that will result in an incomplete product, while everything more than that will result in unnecessary expenses and a waste of time at this point.

Now that you have all the sketches in front of you, as well as the elaborate description of what your product actually needs to be, who your target audiences are, what the values for each of your target audiences are and how you will monetize the product, making valid decisions on the MVP features should be fairly straightforward.

Create a spreadsheet and start preparing the list of the MVP features. At the same time, consider this: your MVP must have a parallel web solution that your business will use for managing and analyzing the data of the main product. We'll get to that part very soon.

Additionally, do not throw all your good ideas away, but rather create a separate sheet for all the other features. Once your main sheet for the MVP is ready, prioritize other features and add a note next to each one explaining what will influence the need for it in the future.

This brings us to metrics. It is crucial to know what data must be tracked and what conversions mean.

DEFINE THE SUB-PRODUCTS THAT ENRICH YOUR MAIN DIGITAL PRODUCT

A set of apps which function in relation to each other as part of one product represents a Solution. For example, a UK-based food delivery business Roofoods Ltd known as Deliveroo has a consumer-facing mobile app, a restaurant-facing web app, a driver-facing mobile app, a business-facing web app, and surely a few other apps. All these apps in conjunction represent a software solution.

Sub-products are software solutions that primarily provide an interface to data, data analytics, business intelligence and content management for the main digital product. Sub-products simply must exist, some may be 3rd party solutions, some may be custom solutions, while some may be a mix of both. Sub-products give you the means to run a business with intelligence and to make knowledgeable business decisions.

Let's explore one of each from the simplest perspective.

Fabric[8]
Fabric is a platform that helps mobile teams build better apps and grow their business by understanding their users. Fabric supports iOS, macOS, tvOS, Android and Unity. It will help you understand how your app is doing, in real-time. Fabric is a Google product.

With Engagement as the main focus, you will be able to get insight into your users and what actions they're taking within your app. With Retention as the secondary focus, you will be able to uncover behaviors that correlate with healthy and unhealthy users.

[8] https://get.fabric.io/ Fabric is currently being integrated into Google Firebase (https://firebase.google.com/) and from March 31, 2020 it will be full integrated.

Even though Fabric will give you insight into your users, their behaviors, and what actions they are taking, Fabric is unaware of the data that flows through your digital product. Let's take GDPR as a popular topic, by which you must be able, upon request, to provide your user with information of what data you are collecting about them, to present them with that data, and be able to delete it. No third party solution will enable you to do so, and therefore, you are legally obligated to be able to do such things. As a result—you must have a sub-product that can manage this requirement.

App Store and Play Store

App Store and Play Store can also be considered sub-products, as they provide you with data about downloads and, most importantly, about finances, if your sales channel goes through in-app purchases.

Likewise, if you use PayPal or Stripe or anything similar as a payment gateway, their systems will give you a full insight into the finances.

However, if you use more than one, cross-referencing data becomes a manual task, a task that will grow and consume even more time and money. Therefore, a custom sub-product needs to be built so that it automates the financial data reports.

Power BI

In terms of cross-referencing data, in the case when data is being stored by your own system or by a 3rd party integrated system, Power BI by Microsoft is a powerful business analytics tool that provides interactive visualizations with self-service business intelligence capabilities, where end users can create reports and dashboards by themselves, without having to depend on information technology staff or database administrators.

Even though Power BI sounds like the top of the food chain solution, it is not, as Power BI is a visualization tool. All of these interesting and useful 3rd party sub-products do not have the means to put the power of data analytics back into the power of your main product, nor can they put all the data together in one bin.

Therefore, certainly do utilize 3rd party solutions, as they will be of great importance to the future of your product and the success of your business, but know that your custom sub-product must be on top of the food chain in regard to all these products.

A major international airport, Heathrow Airport, employs Power BI in the process of pulling data for the purposes of informing their employees about the changes in the airport traffic. This is a necessary step in the staff's preparations for unexpected occurrences at the airport. This usage of data demonstrates Heathrow's ambitions to change the travel experience for the better.

MILESTONE 8 — LEARN HOW WIREFRAMING CAN ENSURE YOUR INVESTMENT AND THE DELIVERY OF YOUR DIGITAL PRODUCT

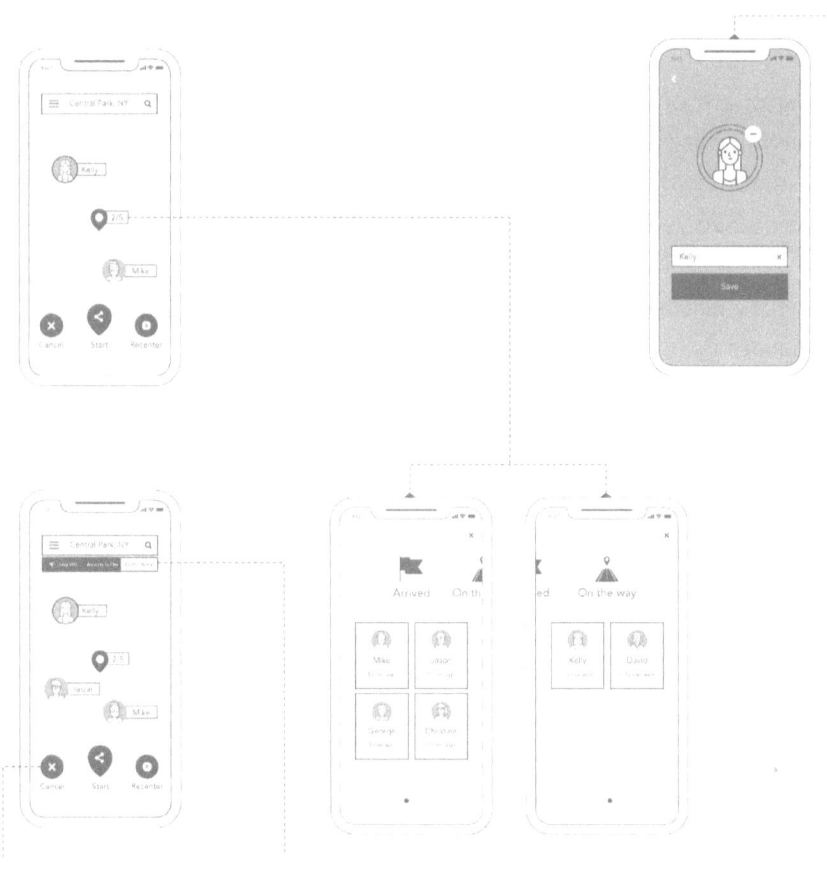

Finally, a true visual representation of the product. Once we have milestones 1 through 7 down, we can finally start producing the documentation for the product–the visual representation of the product that visually fully defines what is being built.

One could argue that sketches are totally sufficient as wireframes, and honestly, most would say those do fulfill wireframe requirements.

So how come they are not? The power of the wireframes is in the details.

Experience has taught me not to leave any details to interpretation or the free will of the developer. Don't think this is a remark against developers, on the contrary, this is only to their benefit, since everything is chewed up to the tiniest detail, all they have to do is do their work as best as they can. Therefore, you optimize the effort of all parties involved in the delivery of the product.

Let's just take the simplest example–the Sign in/Sign up process. What are the requirements and what are the arising questions?

Native Sign up/Login:
1. Email
2. Password

Native Sign up Questions:
1. Do we want an email confirmation field?
2. Do we want a password confirmation field?
3. Do we want the user to verify their email before signing in?
4. Do we want a username at sign up?
5. Do we need any additional data on sign up?
6. We need to indicate that the user's input is validated.

Native Login Questions:
1. What happens if the user forgets their password?
2. What if they forget what email they used?
3. How do they reset the password? What is the process to do so? There are 2-3 common possibilities for that.
4. Do we want to email them a link to sign in without a password?

Facebook Sign up/in Questions:
1. What user permissions are we asking for? Why? What will we do with the data?
2. Once they are authenticated, do we need to collect any more information? At which point do we do this so that we do not bother the user?
3. Can that Facebook-authenticated user also sign in natively? What is the process? If yes, what is the benefit of it?

Wireframes must cover off all of these visually.

In many cases, things do get technical and designers must work alongside the tech team and the product owner to produce wireframes that fulfill both the technical and the product requirements. Even though we do not have these yet, this is the moment they should start preparing. Therefore, this phase initiates the creation of the technical requirements, the functional specification, and of the crucial functional decisions. In the previous phases, we did not care if the user's email was verified, now we do.

This is just the sign up/in process, and it includes so many details while being the simplest feature of the entire product! Can you now see the importance of the wireframes being completed in accordance with my instructions? Are you starting to grasp the importance of functional spec and tech requirements?

Now imagine you do not do all this and you hand it off to developers. This sign up/in process can take as little as one day and as much as ten days to develop. What will happen once they deliver ten times less of what you imagined, even though it was obvious but never specified?

MILESTONE 9 — ELEVEN OBVIOUS DIGITAL PRODUCT FUNCTIONAL SPECIFICATION BENEFITS

While a picture is worth a thousand words, pictures cannot elaborate all functional aspects of the product. Elaborating the wireframes by specifying how things work from both frontend and backend perspectives is priceless—e.g. specifying what a user does when performing an action, elaborating how the system reacts to that and all the processes that are triggered is essential—do you really want to leave it to a developer, whose core knowledge is to code things and make them work, to define on the go what needs to be done there? Then he/she is the one that presents it to you? Would you specify all of this once it becomes needed? On the go?

The key deliverables:

1. All functionalities fully elaborated from A to Z to the tiniest details. This is exactly what is going to be built, nothing more, nothing less. This document leaves nothing unanswered and does not leave place for interpretation.
2. The client reviews the document and confirms the first key delivery.
3. The wireframes are adjusted to cover details that are realized during this phase.

There is a factor of experience and knowledge of course, and with an agile approach, many things can be left untold and unspecified at the end, but do you have the time, the money and the resources to handle it? How often can you deliver a project with unknown delivery estimates? Even the teams with unlimited funding stick to something, that's how they got there in the first place. Unless you work as a scientist in a research institute, you better hold on to something solid.

Functional Specification can be delivered in phases, so that it follows the product roadmap. Therefore, specifying only the upcoming sprint (phase, milestone, however you call it…) will suffice in some cases (like in a more agile approach with flexible funding resources), while a fully specified product is required for projects with fixed time and cost requirements.

11 Obvious Digital Product Functional Specification Benefits are:

1. Nothing is left to interpretation.
2. The delivery timeline is precise.
3. The delivery cost is precise.
4. Miscommunication is avoided.
5. Who-said-what is avoided.
6. There is a clear line of responsibility.
7. All Stakeholders can focus on their primary activities.
8. The product will be delivered.
9. The product will be delivered as required.
10. The product will reach its full potential.
11. The business will have a high-quality tool to operate with.

MILESTONE 10 — TURN THE TECHNICAL DOCUMENTATION INTO A VALUABLE SUPPLEMENT OF YOUR PRODUCT DEVELOPMENT ROUTINE

In today's agile and lean tech world where everything is activated on the go and everything is instant, my 12-milestone methodology sounds like an unnecessary burden, while the preparation of the technical documentation could be considered madness. For that reason, let's turn the Technical Documentation into a valuable supplement rather than a boring overhead in your product development routine.

There are three key influences that define the need for the Technical Documentation, and a certain level of detail is required. Sometimes a product requires a fully blown Technical Documentation, sometimes there's a need for something called the Technical Requirements Document, while sometimes there is no need for the documentation. It is important to grasp when each case can be applied the most.

.

When a New Digital Product represents a tech innovation or is an emerging tech product, there is an obvious dependency on the tech solution, and how better to define what is to be developed if not with the Technical Documentation? Functional Specification in this case is for non-tech people to understand what is going on, but without the Technical Documentation, there is a lack of evidence or guidance regarding what is to be developed.

The entire 12-milestone methodology must be adjusted appropriately so as to focus on technology, where the end-user functionality is a business case. Yes, you got that right—much like when a pharmaceutical giant launches a new medicine, the medicine is an emerging product, while what the medicine is for, how it is being used, to whom it will be prescribed, what its pros and cons are and millions of other functional features are the business case. It is exactly the same with tech innovation/emerging tech—much like the medicine must be properly defined, i.e. what goes in it, in which form and in which ratio and a million other things as well (since all of this is what defines it), in the same way is the new tech product defined by how it is constructed, how it works, what its pieces are, in what form and in what ratio and also by millions of other things.

When a New Digital Product has specific Technical Requirements that make it viable, there is a very specific dependency on the Technical Documentation, and in this case, as I already stated—the Technical Requirement Document. It's common sense really. In this scenario, the minimal requirement to make your product viable is the documentation of those specifics, so that whoever develops it does so as specified. Even if you are a developer yourself, specify it, document it, keep the document updated, for this technical requirement is what gives your product feasibility to succeed, it is good to have it documented.

When a New Digital Product does not have anything specific regarding the Technical solution, there is no need for the Technical Documentation. Worst case scenario—some basic Technical Requirements are good to have, depending on who will deliver the product for you. If you are working with a team that you have a track record with, or you are building in-house and have your way of working and developing already in place, or you are developing yourself, there is no need for the documentation, and yes, in that case it is an overhead.

Regardless, why not secure your digital product investment by specifying and documenting all core dependencies that will make sure your digital product sees the light of day and that it works and performs as required and needed in order to give your business a feasible chance for success.

Business development is business development, marketing is marketing, but in order to get into the position needed for developing your business and for marketing the product, the product must be properly built.

That is the fact that is above all others in its level of importance—if the product is not properly designed, engineered, built and deployed, nothing else can function smoothly. The product must not fail you nor your business.

MILESTONE 11 — THE MOST IMPORTANT ASPECTS OF DIGITAL PRODUCT EXECUTION EFFORT ESTIMATES

TIME & MONEY

% 25% 50% 75% 100%

YOUR DIGITAL PRODUCT EXECUTION

Regardless of how you would execute the delivery of your digital product, in-house or by contracting, the value of estimating the delivery efforts is essential to the two parameters that are most relevant to your business – time and money. Additionally, estimated cloud hosting costs for dev, test and production environments are good to have, as well as the minimum for the expected support engagement if the product requires such efforts.

I keep stating that planning is everything. The project management methodology, as agile and as lean as it gets, should not influence the fact that solid metrics must be in place adjacent to the execution of a digital product. Even when contracting a team on a TnM basis, expectations should be set for at least the next delivery iteration.

Time and materials (aka TnM) is a standard phrase in a contract for product development or any other piece of work in which the employer agrees to pay the contractor based upon the time spent by the contractor's employees and subcontractor's employees on performing the work, and for materials used in the development, no matter how much work is required to complete the construction. Time and Materials is generally used in projects in which it is not possible to accurately estimate the size of the project, or when it is expected that the project requirements will most likely change.

Now that your entire product blueprint is ready, it is easy to prepare extremely precise execution estimates. I could argue that the risks for the delivery of a digital product have been made obsolete, and that is true in 99% of the cases. That one percent refers to an edge case that very few people in this world can find themselves in, and it concerns technical innovations made in such a way that there is nothing like it on the market, it has not been executed before, so there are no metrics against which you can measure the estimates for execution or even know if it is possible to deliver the product at all.

There are ways around this that can leverage the risks to acceptable levels, but I would be going off topic if I were to deep dive any further.

Therefore – yes, the execution estimates are prepared based on the metrics of someone having delivered something like this or many pieces of something like this before. Whether it is your own experience or your colleague's experience or of someone from the tech branch that you employ or know, it is up to you to choose, all the while making sure the estimates are realistic and taking into consideration the experience and knowledge required to deliver the digital product.

Estimates are expressed through the effort required to deliver the entire digital product – all the types of "actions" required, to say the least. Effort is represented by the number of days (it can be a fraction of a day) that it takes a single resource (developer, designer, whoever…) to deliver a chunk of functionality. Even when it comes to agile methodologies such as Scrum, time and team size when talking about deliveries, they are directly translatable to resource-per-day effort.

Estimates should be broken down into areas such as Project initialization effort, Design effort, Backend (API) effort, Frontend Presentation Layer effort, Frontend Functional implementation effort, Quality Assurance and Management effort.

Project initialization effort

This is the effort required to get the project on its feet. Here I classify this as the initial effort required for the execution team to analyze the requirements, for them to engage in a few meetings with you in order to get things started, but most importantly – System Design, Database Design, and Software Architecture.

Design effort

This is the effort reserved for all of the following: Branding, Visual Identity, UI design, UX design, Responsive design and Physical Product Design (IoT).

Backend (API) effort

This is the effort required for the backend development team to deliver the API based on the already defined System Design and Software Architecture.

Frontend Presentation Layer effort

This is the effort required to deliver the non-functional frontend product based of the Design effort deliverables.

Frontend Functional implementation effort

This is the effort reserved for bridging the gap between the API and the Presentation layer – basically, it is a coding effort required to make the Presentation layer communicate with the API and make the product functional.

Quality Assurance

This is the effort required to ensure the quality of deliverables by automated and manual testing of the product features as well as to ensure the quality of the Presentation layer implementation that is to be pixel-perfect as per designs.

Management effort

This is the effort required to manage the project from Product, Project, Technical and DevOps perspectives.

Based on all of the above, a simple example of a chunk of functionality for a Sign up feature for your digital product: Design effort (effort required to design UI/UX of the form); Backend effort (effort required to deliver API endpoints and business logic that will sign up a user); Frontend Presentation Layer effort (effort required to style the form on a Web or Mobile interface); Frontend Functional Implementation effort (effort required to bridge the gap between Backend API end-points and styled frontend ones); Quality Assurance (effort required to confirm required functionality works and performs as visually and functionally specified).

MILESTONE 12 — THE IMPORTANCE OF THE STATEMENT OF WORK FOR THE DELIVERY OF A DIGITAL PRODUCT

The Statement of Work (SOW) is a document routinely used to define deliverables and timelines for a vendor providing services to a client.

I advise having the SOW prepared even when executing a delivery in-house, as all the risks that are involved when contracting someone external coexist with not taking the same precautions with an in-house execution. The approach should be precisely the same with the same goals – ensure the delivery as specified, within the scope, and within the time and cost estimates.

The SOW should include detailed requirements as well. Since there is a full product blueprint based on all the milestones completed so far, Wireframes, Functional Specification and Technical Requirements are the detailed requirements that are included in the SOW.

The SOW should also incorporate a timeline and the cost of your delivery. This is not a problem – the execution effort estimates are already prepared. Logically, the cost of the delivery exists when delivering in-house and it is only calculated by the internal cost, not by the external cost.

Any specific requirements that are not part of the product definition should be stated here, such as tech stack, design tools, collaboration/management tools, deadlines, reporting, working hours and similar.

THE EXECUTION

The IT industry has changed substantially in the past couple of years due to a massive increase in its services' demand. This constant and ever-increasing demand for developers has interfered with the IT market in a way that freelancers and software development agencies can be found on every corner, leading to a decreasing percentage of available highly experienced senior engineers. As both the supply and the demand will continue to grow over the next decade, with the demand always exponentially higher than the supply, this fact will remain relevant.

Looking to outsource is no longer just a quest for the cheaper cost of the delivery, but rather a simple need to obtain resources that can deliver, in which case the quality of the delivery is a major factor. This fact has obviously led to an increased cost of all the services required to deliver a fully functional product—not only of the software devs' and any sort of engineers', but also of the designers', testers', dev-ops', managers', consultants', everyone's really.

However, the cost is only one of the two main factors, and the other one is much more important!

Five years ago, the mass majority of companies that wished to outsource software delivery service operations mostly went to India. While India remains a major outsourcing country, nowadays Eastern Europe is full of outsourcing centers.

There are two kinds of value—the value of money and the value of something actually being delivered as required. A company that outsources must not take into consideration only the financial savings (the value of money)—those savings must bring the same or at least similar results (the value of delivery). If you don't deliver the product, your savings are worth nothing.

FROM IDEA TO DIGITAL PRODUCT: FINAL NOTE

Thank you for getting this far with reading my book. I hope I have given you valuable information through it. Maybe the book ends here, but if you took your idea on this journey, that means you now have your own chapter to write. I wish you all the best!

To conclude, let's recap the most important aspects of each of the milestones.

The 1st milestone: Product definition

Know exactly what the heart and the soul of your future product are. Product description must be comprehensive and elaborated, even to a level that explains why each of the functionalities is required. Everything must be done with a reason in order to prevent yourself from investing into something that does not have a reason. While reasons may change over time, taking notes of your decisions and thoughts provides unprecedented value for future product development and business growth.

The key deliverables:

1. Elaborate and describe your digital product idea in writing
2. Name the product
3. Write down your idea in one precise sentence
4. Question the idea

The 2nd milestone: Define target audienceS and recognize the obvious segmentation within

Know exactly who the buyers are. What is specific about them? How does this product appeal to them? How does the business adapt to them? Is there a common model that can represent the first version that is somewhat appealing to all target audience segments which would help release it sooner rather than later?

The key deliverables:

1. Elaborate and assume the target audience
2. If you are they key actor of your target audience, recognize who you are in your story and extract new target audiences
3. Define Who will use your product, How/When and Why
4. Recognize the obvious segmentation within each of the Target Audiences
5. Elaborate to yourself the 4 main premises of Milestone 2:
6. Requirements for the vision of the MVP version
7. Who do you recognize as the major target audience?
8. Start planning how to approach the target audience
9. Start thinking of the MVP vs the next phases of development against the Target Audience layout

The 3rd milestone: Define the main value propositions

Knowledge is value. Knowing the value that the product will bring to consumers is crucial for product concepting. Based on the facts of who the target audience is, you have a foundation needed to define the main value propositions. How does the product bring value to its consumers and how does it change their work and life?

The key deliverables:

1. Generalize the Target Audiences into obvious groups
2. Define the Primary and Secondary Main Value Propositions for each Target Audience group
3. Conclude if the values for each group match or differ

The 4th milestone: Define how the product makes money

This tends to be obvious at the beginning, however, team brainstorming brings out a lot of barriers and new potential revenue streams. If all possible financial models are already prepared, how clearly do these models reflect on the business plans and the product that is evolving during this process? What if the business plans change, how does the product react to the changes? What does one need to be able to adapt to those changes?

The key deliverables:

1. Identify if the product is freemium or premium
2. Identify the free features (if any)
3. Identify if your MVP should already offer premium features
4. Identify the premium features (if any)

The 5th milestone: Sketch the concept

The visual representation of an idea speaks a 1000 words and craves further creativity. The fastest way to present something, to brainstorm and to come up with the concept is sketching by hand. It allows you to think fast, to progress rapidly… It cannot be done prior to milestones 1 through 4, as they feed you the foundation for creating the concept. These are the first visible results that everyone can understand and discuss. It allows for quick iteration and advancement based on a solid background.

The key deliverables:

1. A rough sketch of the initial vision of the core product (MVP)

The 6th milestone: Incrementally improve the concept

Get the best out of the idea in the moment all the creativity is in its maximum. This is the point in time everything can still be revised until every stakeholder is satisfied, while invested time and money are in its minimum. Nothing went too far, it went to the point where revisions are time and cost effective.

The key deliverables:

1. A rough sketch of a fully blown product based on the premises from the 1st milestone and further expansion of the idea and the features laid out in milestones 2 through 5 (to the level of acceptable effort and imagination).

The 7th milestone: Realize your delivery phases and delivery phase influences

Compare everything that the product could be against the core idea, realize what is really necessary, what has no purpose, what has no purpose just yet, and in which phase the purpose will be generated. We have the concept now, we can realize what the delivery phases can be, what their order of priority is, what is a must, what is decoration that may or may not be needed and when and how you can know that.

The key deliverables:

1. A definitive decision on what the MVP will consist of
2. A brief description of each of the screens that visually define the functionality

The 8th milestone: Proceed with wireframing

Finally, a true visual representation of the product. Once we have milestones 1 through 7 down, we can finally start producing the documentation for the product—the visual representation of the product that visually fully defines what is being built.

The key deliverables:

1. Fully blown wireframes including even the tiniest details of the MVP

The 9th milestone: Prepare the functional specification

While a picture is worth a thousand words, pictures cannot elaborate all functional aspects of the product. Elaborating the wireframes by specifying how things work from both frontend and backend perspectives is priceless—e.g. specifying what a user does when performing an action, and elaborating how the system reacts to that and what are all the processes that are triggered is essential—do you really want to leave it to a developer, whose core knowledge is to code things and make them work, to define on the go what needs to be done there? Then he/she is the one that presents it to you? Would you specify all of this once it becomes needed? On the go?

The key deliverables:

1. All functionalities fully elaborated from A to Z to the tiniest details. This is exactly what is going to be built, nothing more, nothing less. This document leaves nothing unanswered and does not leave place for interpretation
2. The client reviews the document and confirms the first key delivery
3. The wireframes are adjusted to cover details that are realized during this phase

The 10th milestone: Prepare the technical requirements

This is often not needed, and for the majority of functionalities it never is, but if the implementation is specific in order to be able to accommodate technical requirements for other goals that are not visible from the functional specification, the technical specification must elaborate what needs to be done, to set the direction in which it is going to be done, and to elaborate why it needs to be done.

The key deliverables:

1. The elaboration of the requirements that make this product technically viable
2. The technical requirements that must be utilized as defined in order for the project to properly function

The 11th milestone: Prepare the Statement of Work

Clearly indicate the requirements for the execution of the idea. While the wireframes and specs define it, they do not indicate the production requirements. At this point, you will finally elaborate your documentation in a way that you express the requirements to the development team in terms of your expectations. The scope of work may include requirements for the design, the backend, the integration, the technology and cloud infrastructure, etc…

The key deliverables:

1. A list of all the requirements from the technical delivery team
2. A list of all the requirements for the project to go live
3. A list of all the requirements for future support of the project

The 12th milestone: Prepare the execution estimates

Know the time and the cost of your delivery—it is easy now that you have everything chewed up. Based on all of the above, strict estimates of the defined work can be made. You can know exactly how much time it is needed to deliver something. At this point, all the risks of the estimates going wrong can be made, and the index of said risks can be defined. At this point, asking the dev companies to give you a quote is 100% on the safe side.

The key deliverables:

1. The effort breakdown for the delivery featured in man/days (MVP)
2. The timeline estimates by phases (design, system design, software architecture, development, QA, deployments)
3. Estimated costs for production system operations
4. Support requirements

Finally, enjoy the journey!

ABOUT THE AUTHOR

Ivan Trajkovic is the founder of three IT companies: Ivan Agency, Engineers and Engineers London. Funnily enough, his initials are IT.

After having lived through years of war and poverty, he graduated from Nova Southeastern University with B.Sc. in CIS in 2004. Ivan is among a handful of his generation in his home country Serbia to win the generation's dream of a full basketball scholarship at a university in the States.

He loves breathing life into digital products. In his successful management so far, there are more than two hundred digital products to show for it, hundreds more to come and he wants to create value by sharing his passion, knowledge, experience and future endeavors.

"Concepting, building and innovating a digital product is like raising a child in a way, and there is no better feeling than that! Do not forget—raise it well and it will love you back and look after you…"

Stay informed. Join the discussion.

Visit ivan.agency

Follow @ivan_agency on Twitter

Find us on YouTube, Podcast, LinkedIn, Facebook, Instagram, Medium

www.ingramcontent.com/pod-product-compliance
Lightning Source LLC
Chambersburg PA
CBHW021849170526
45157CB00007B/2997